THIS BOOK
BELONGS TO :

____

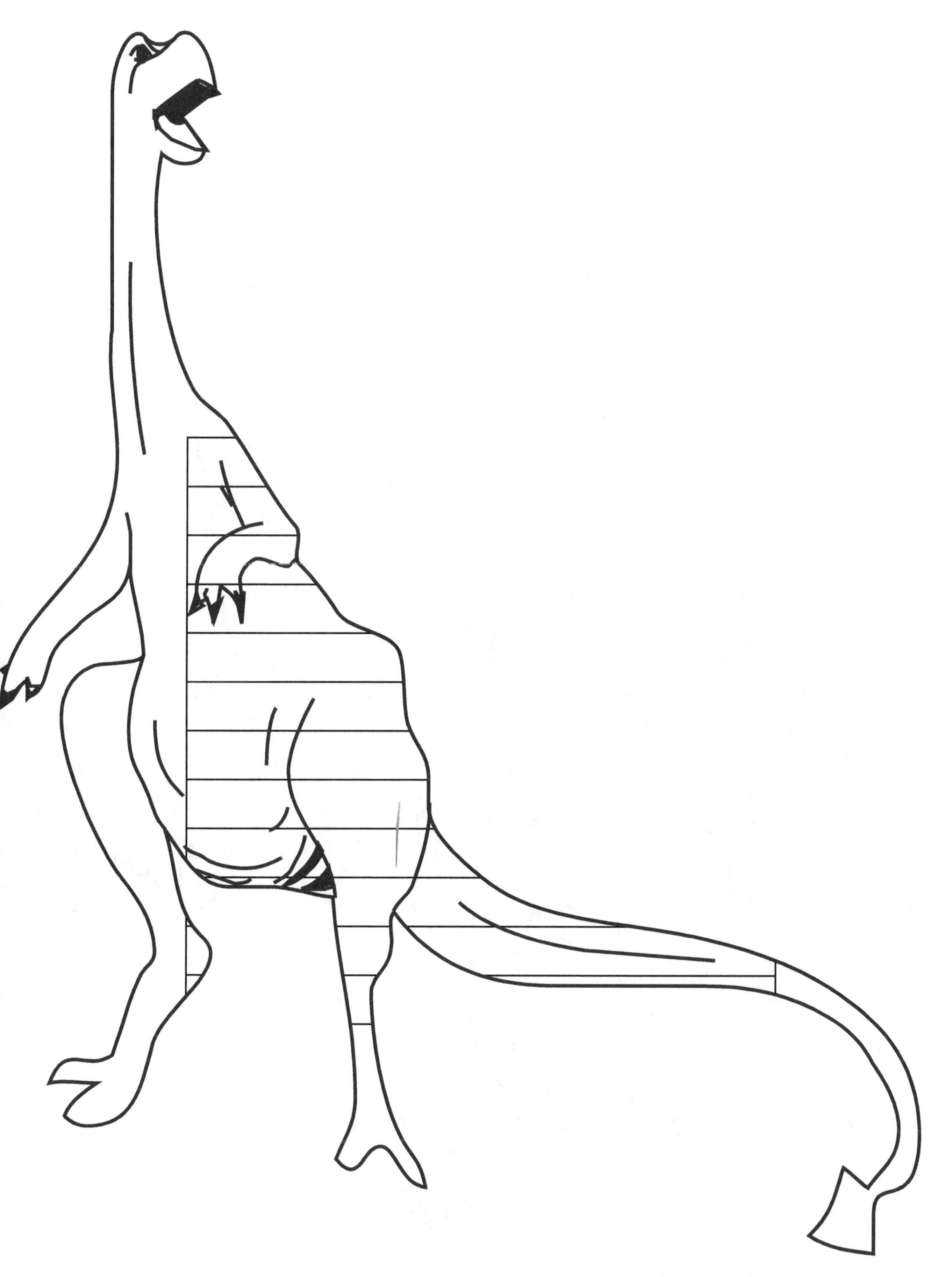

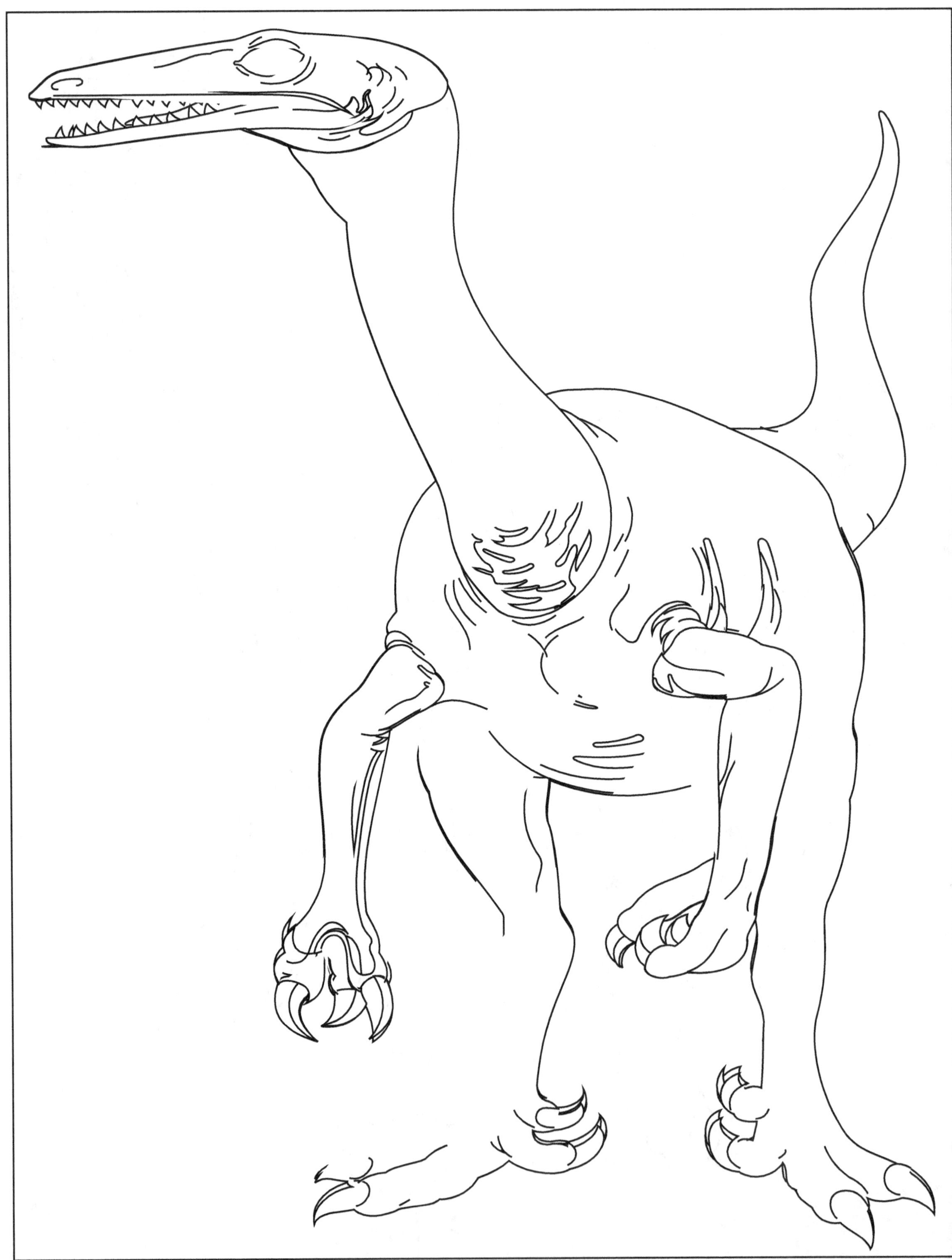

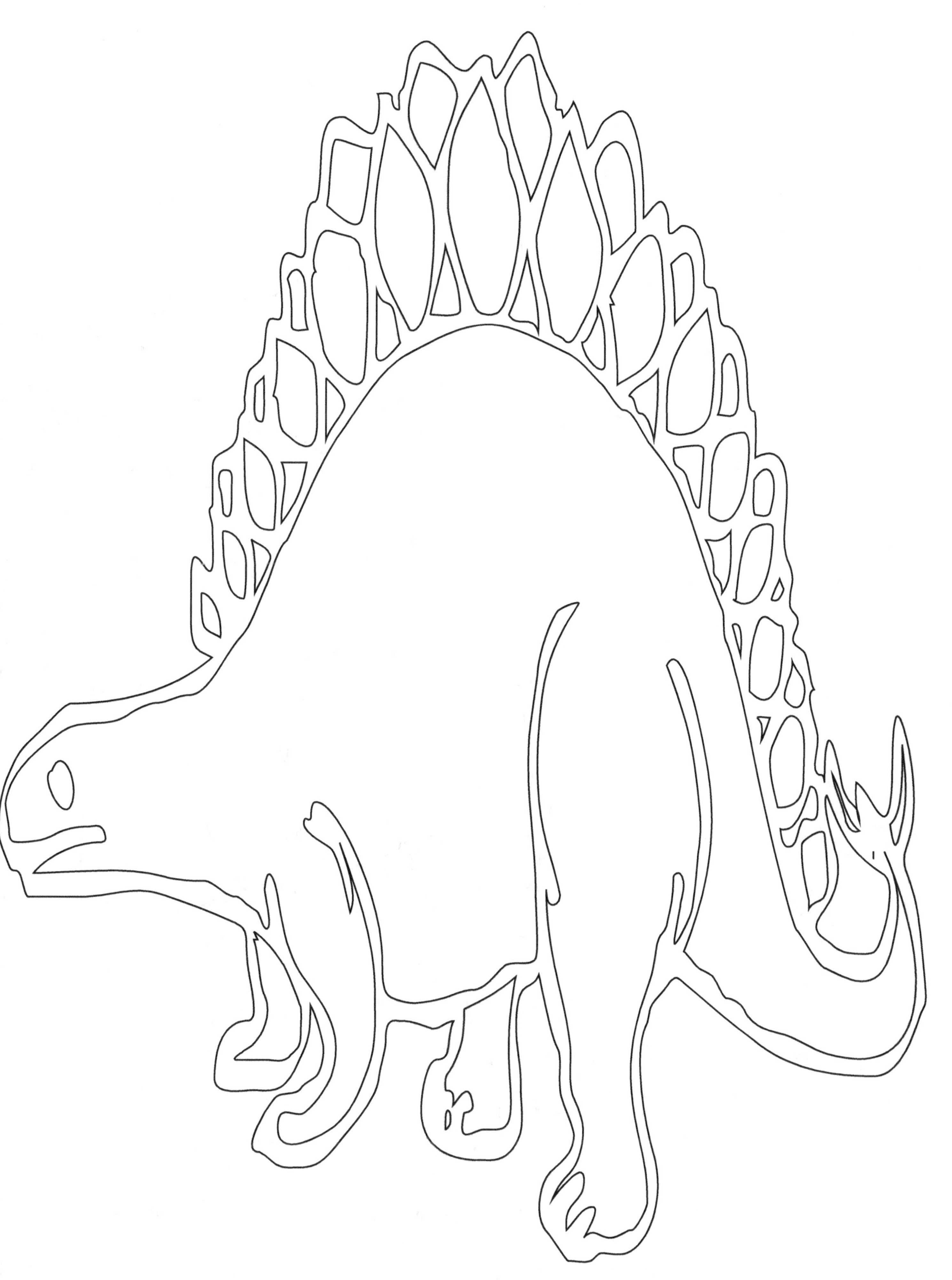

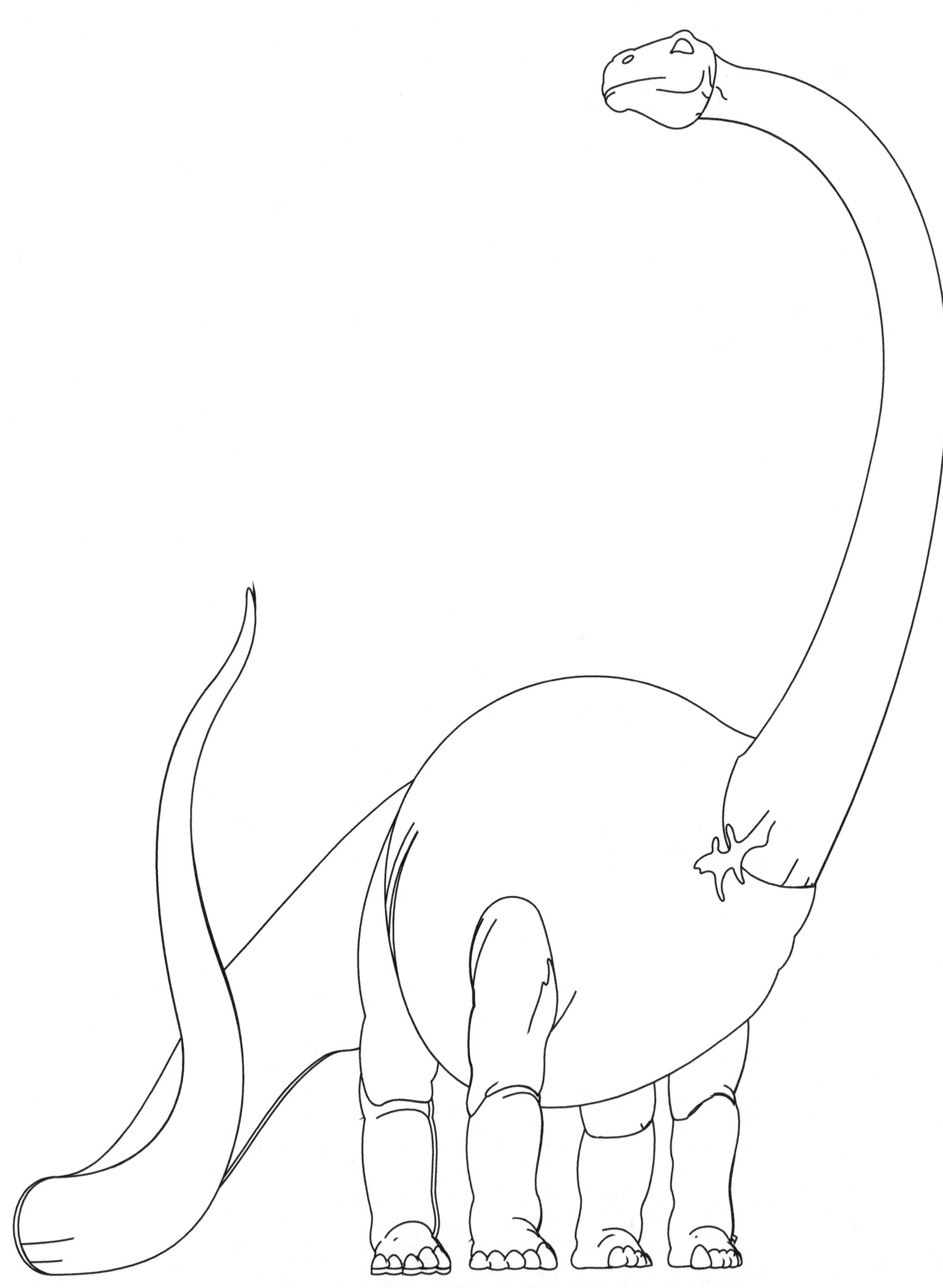

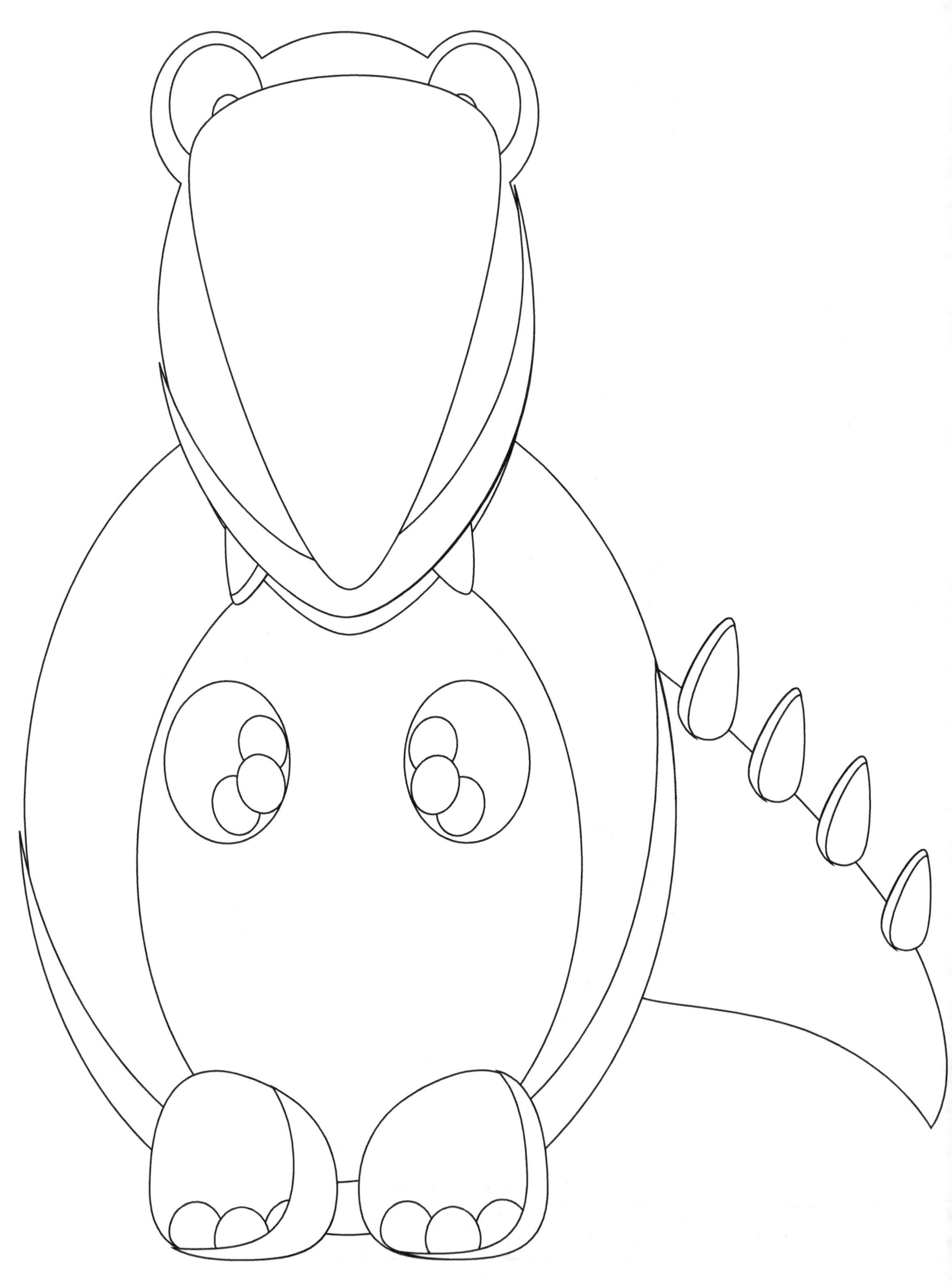

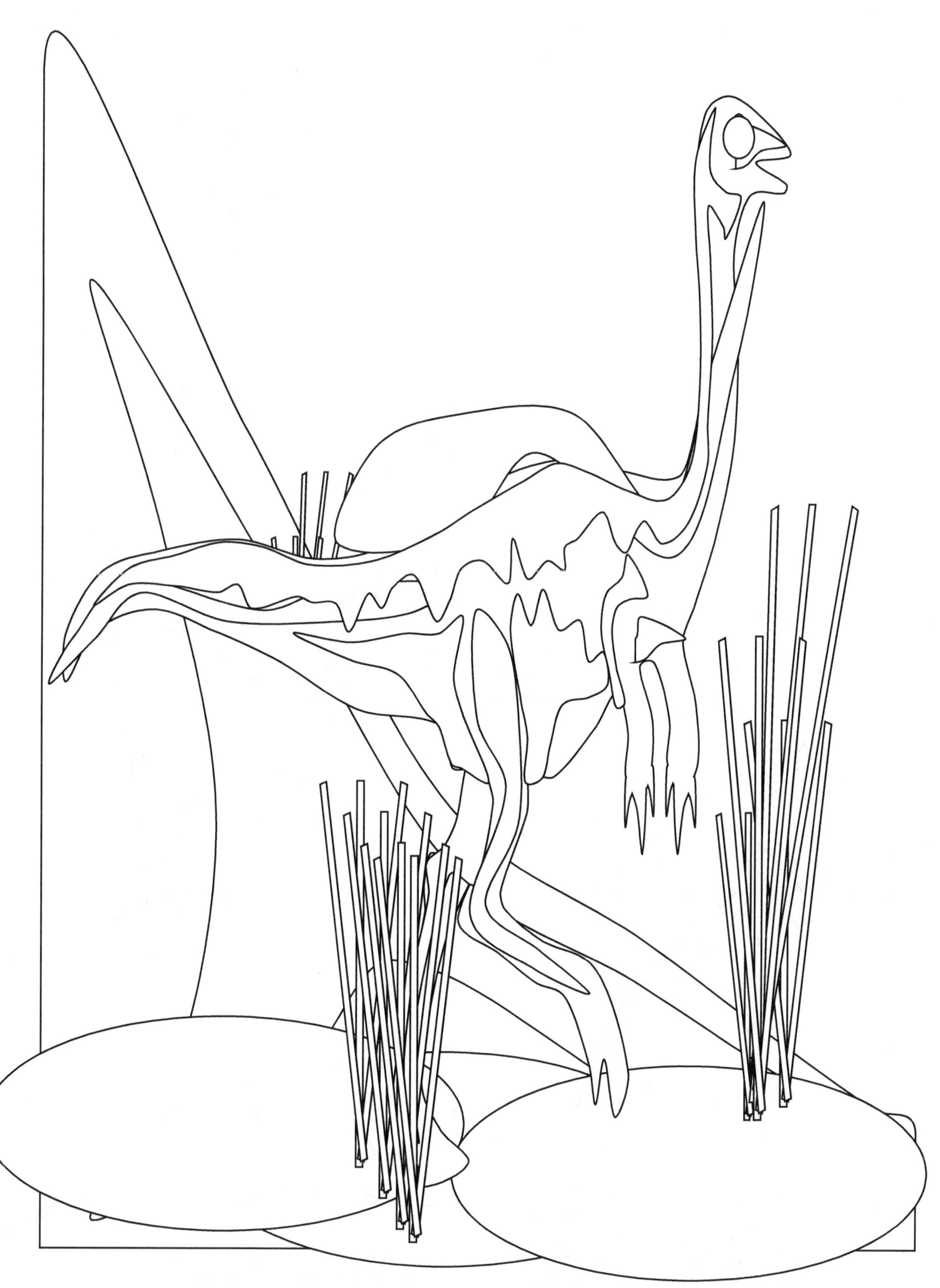